Leading IT with Purpose

Letters on Using ITIL to Build Teams, Trust, and Tech That Works

A. H. Robinson

Published by Harborview Publishing, LLC

ISBN: 9798349513602
First Edition

Printed in the United States of America

This book is a work of nonfiction. Names, companies, and experiences referenced are either used with permission or are the product of the author's professional experience. Any resemblance to actual persons or situations is purely coincidental and unintentional.

Table of Contents

Acknowledgments

This book is for my family. Without the support of my wife, Brenna, this book would not have been possible. She helped motivate me to write the book and provided support throughout the process. Ashley and Sydni, my daughters, are my inspiration and most incredible supporters. To my sons-in-law, Tim and Noah, thank you for your support and for golfing when I needed a mental break. I could not have done it without you all.

About the Author

Dr. Tony Robinson is a seasoned IT leader, educator, and mentor known for his clarity, discipline, and grounded approach to leadership. With more than 20 years of experience spanning higher education and enterprise technology, he's built a reputation for helping teams navigate complex problems with focus and purpose.

Throughout his career, as a systems engineer, director, CIO, and Educator, Dr. Robinson has led initiatives that blend operational excellence with long-term vision. His calm, thoughtful leadership has earned the trust of stakeholders in high-stakes environments where precision and people both matter.

What sets Dr. Robinson apart is his belief that leadership isn't just about technical knowledge; it's about how you think. He brings that philosophy to life through his writing, teaching, and mentorship, helping others sharpen their thinking, communicate with integrity, and act with intention.

Leading IT with Purpose: Letters on Using ITIL to Build Teams, Trust, and Tech That Works is his second book, following *The Disciplined Mind.* In this collection of real-world letters, he equips fellow leaders with the tools and mindset to lead with purpose, not theory. Through stories, questions, and practical frameworks, Dr. Robinson challenges readers to lead from where they are—with clarity, courage, and conviction.

Preface

I didn't set out to write another leadership book. I set out to write the one I wish I had when I first stepped into the fire.

The one that could have saved me from learning everything the hard way. The one that didn't speak in frameworks and buzzwords, but in real stories, real decisions, and the quiet tension of trying to lead well in complex, high-stakes environments.

Over the years, I've sat in boardrooms, classrooms, and server rooms—and in every one of them, I've seen a pattern. People aren't struggling because they don't know enough. They're struggling because they're overloaded, under-aligned, and constantly asked to deliver outcomes in systems that were never built to support clarity.

This book is my answer to that.

It was born not just from one project, but from a career of hard-earned insights, missed steps, course corrections, and moments of clarity. It's a bridge between my two callings: leading technology and teaching people how to lead it better.

If *The Disciplined Mind* was about building a foundation, this is about forward motion. It's about turning good intentions into trusted systems. Ideas into impact. It's about leadership that holds.

So before you dive in, here's what I'll ask you: Don't just read this. Wrestle with it. Mark it up. Test it. Bring it into your next conversation. Let it be a sounding board as you lead your team forward—with clarity, integrity, and purpose.

Thanks for stepping into this with me.

Introduction: From Chaos to Clarity – Why These Letters Matter

Dear Reader,

Let me guess—you didn't pick up this book looking for fluff. You're not here for buzzwords, generic strategies, or theoretical leadership advice that sounds good but does nothing. You're here because you want to lead better. Build smarter. And create something that works, something people can believe in.

So, let's start with the truth: leadership today isn't getting easier.

Whether you're leading a tech team, managing change, or trying to earn trust across a fast-moving organization, you're navigating constant pressure, complexity, and noise. Every week brings another new tool, another broken process, another deadline with unclear expectations. And in the middle of all that, you're expected to inspire people.

Sound familiar?

I've been there—more than once. Early in my career, I believed that the right strategy or system could solve anything. If I just picked the perfect platform, nailed the rollout plan, or added one more KPI, I'd finally get ahead. But every time I "checked the boxes," I still felt like something was missing.

We were delivering projects, sure. But were we making an impact? Were we earning trust? Were we building something people *used*, *loved*, and *valued*?

The answer wasn't always yes.

And that's when I realized: outstanding leadership isn't about control. It's about connections.

That's where this book began.

Why Letters?

This isn't a traditional playbook. It's a conversation. A series of letters written from one leader to another—from someone who's been in the trenches to someone walking into the fire now.

Each chapter is a real-world reflection from my time leading the Aurora project. This complex digital transformation effort taught me more about leadership, trust, and simplicity than any textbook ever could. These stories aren't filtered. They're not sugarcoated. They're honest accounts of what worked, what didn't, and what I wish I had known sooner.

But more than that, these letters are a blueprint for building something better.

What You'll Learn

You won't find a rigid framework or cookie-cutter roadmap here. Instead, you'll find something far more powerful and principles *that scale with you.*

Here's what we'll cover together:

- How to define value in a way that matters to your stakeholders.
- Why starting where you are can save you from wasting time, money, and momentum.
- How to build progress that lasts—by listening early and adjusting often.
- What real collaboration looks like when it's built on visibility and trust.
- Why simplifying processes makes you more credible, not less technical.
- How to step back and think system-wide, not siloed.

- When to automate, and when to pause and optimize.
- What it means to lead with purpose—and how that one choice changes everything.

These aren't abstract ideas. They're grounded in lived experience. They're what took my team from scrambling to respected, from overlooked to indispensable.

Who This Is For

This book is for anyone trying to lead something that matters.

You might be a CIO stepping into a new role. A project manager navigating cross-functional chaos. A team lead is trying to accomplish more with fewer resources. Or maybe you're just someone tired of the noise, ready to create work that works.

Whatever your title, if you want to:

- Build systems people use
- Win trust across teams
- Communicate with clarity, not jargon
- Move from reactive to strategic

…then you're in the right place.

A Quick Word on Tone

These letters are direct—but never cold. They're practical—but not preachy. They're about the human side of leadership—the messy, meaningful, "figure it out as you go" kind that shapes culture.

If you're looking for buzzwords or overly polished case studies, this probably isn't your book. But if you're ready to hear the voice of someone who's been where you are—who's stumbled, learned, and led through it—then let's go.

How to Use This Book

Read it in order. Or don't. Skim the headers. Mark up the margins. Come back to the parts that resonate with where you are now.

It's structured for action. Each letter stands on its own—but together, they tell a story. A journey from noise to clarity. From systems to solutions. From doing work to leading change.

At the end of each one, you'll find:

Reflection Questions

These help you stop and think. They'll guide you to unpack what the lesson means in *your* world—your team, your work, your leadership style. Use them to journal, kick off team discussions, or challenge your following project review.

Tools for Action

These are the do-now prompts. Checklists. Playbook ideas. They're meant to help you *practice* what you just read. You can apply them tomorrow—or even today. Whether it's simplifying a process, sharing visibility, or revisiting your team's purpose, these tools are your leadership accelerators.

Put It into Practice

The goal isn't to finish the book. The goal is to transform your leadership approach. Every tool, every question, and every story is designed to help you move from insight to execution. From theory to traction.

Take what resonates. Try it with your team. Adjust what doesn't fit. Make it yours.

Who This Is For

This book is for anyone trying to lead something that matters.

You might be a CIO stepping into a new role. A project manager navigating cross-functional chaos. A team lead is trying to accomplish more with the same resources. Or maybe you're just someone tired of the noise, ready to create work that works.

Whatever your title, if you want to:

- Build systems people use
- Win trust across teams
- Communicate with clarity, not jargon
- Move from reactive to strategic

…then you're in the right place.

The Bottom Line

You don't need to be perfect to lead well. You don't need to be an expert in everything to build something excellent. You need to care enough to keep going. To stay curious. To lead with heart.

If that's you, then these letters are for you.

Welcome to *Leading IT with Purpose: Letters on Using ITIL to Build Teams, Trust, and Tech That Works.*

Let's lead better—together.

With respect and belief in what you're building,

A Fellow Leader

Letter 1: The Aurora Case

You and I haven't met, but I've walked in your shoes. I know what it feels like to carry the weight of technology decisions that can either unlock potential or stall progress. I've sat in those early morning leadership meetings, feeling the pressure to fix things yesterday while still figuring out where even to start today.

Let me take you back to a moment to share an experience from the past with you.

When I took over as CIO at a mid-sized organization, we'll call it Aurora Inc., I started with a simple goal: listen before leading. I scheduled sit-downs with every department head to ask four questions:

How can my team create value for you?

What services are critical to your team?

What's not working?

What would make it better?

The answers were strikingly consistent. Each department had its own vital documents, links, and forms, but there was no central place for anyone to find them. Employees were constantly calling, emailing, and chasing down files. Productivity was leaking through the cracks of a disorganized system.

So, I turned to my team. We had the necessary infrastructure, including file servers and department folders. But no one outside IT knew how to navigate them. We could have trained every employee to memorize file paths, but I knew we needed a more innovative solution.

That's when we pitched the idea of a centralized intranet. One intuitive hub for everything essential. It wasn't groundbreaking tech. It was just what people needed. Practical. Fast. Frictionless.

From that point on, we committed to making every decision aligned with value. Not shiny tools. Not IT for IT's sake. Real value. For real people.

In each letter ahead, I will walk you through how we applied that mindset using the ITIL guiding principles. We didn't just build a tool; we changed how the organization worked together. You'll see how each principle helped us focus, simplify, collaborate, and ultimately deliver something that mattered.

Here's my hope for you:

That you lead not just with expertise, but with empathy. That you chase value, not perfection. That you become the kind of IT leader people trust to make their work better.

So, let's get into it. The following letter will introduce you to the ITIL framework, which has shaped the way I lead.

You've got this.

All the best,

A Fellow Leader

Letter 2: Overview of ITIL

Dear Future Leader,

Now that you've seen the spark that kicked off our Aurora project, it's time to talk about the framework that turned our good intentions into tangible, lasting outcomes. I'm talking about ITIL—the Information Technology Infrastructure Library.

I know, the name sounds like something you'd find collecting dust in a back-office binder. But here's the truth: when used right, ITIL isn't a set of rules. It's a mindset; a set of guiding principles that can bring clarity when everything feels messy.

Before I adopted ITIL, I approached each new project as if it were a brand-new puzzle—starting from scratch, reinventing the wheel, and often exhausting myself and my team. We were working hard, but not always smart.

Then I found ITIL's seven guiding principles:

1. Focus on value
2. Start where you are
3. Progress iteratively with feedback
4. Collaborate and promote visibility
5. Think and work holistically
6. Keep it simple and practical
7. Optimize and automate

Each one sounds simple on paper, but when you bring them together, they form a powerful lens through which to lead. For me, these principles gave structure to my instincts. They helped me gain buy-in faster, make better decisions, and lead projects that not only finished but also worked effectively.

Let's rewind for a second. ITIL started back in the 1980s as a UK government initiative. Over time, it evolved into a global framework for IT service management. The version I lean on today—ITIL 4—is modern, agile, and tailored for the kind of fast-paced, high-pressure environments we all work in now.

Why does ITIL matter to you?

Because, as a leader, your job isn't just to "manage IT." It's to bridge the gap between IT and business. To turn systems into outcomes. Tools into solutions. ITIL helps you do that by focusing not on the tech, but on the value the tech delivers.

The seven guiding principles are your leadership north stars. They will help you:

- Make smart, value-driven decisions
- Improve continuously, not just occasionally
- Collaborate across departments, not in silos
- Design usable solutions

They've shaped how I lead my teams, structured my strategy, and defined success.

No jargon. No theory. Just real-world application.

So, if you've ever felt like your team is doing a lot but not moving forward, or if you've struggled to explain to leadership why IT matters, these subsequent letters are for you.

You don't need to memorize ITIL. You need to understand how to live it.

With respect,

A Fellow Leader

Letter 3: The Real Meaning of Value

Dear Fellow Leader,

If I could sit across from you right now, coffee in hand, I'd ask you one thing:

What does *value* mean to you?

Not to your tools. Not to your team. To *you*, as a leader responsible for delivering outcomes that matter.

That question changed everything for me.

One of the first ITIL principles is ***Focus on Value***. It sounds obvious. But in practice? It's the difference between building something people use and building something people rely on.

Back at Aurora, before we did anything else, I made it a priority to understand what value looked like to our stakeholders. I didn't assume. I asked. I sat with department heads and frontline staff and asked them what got in their way, what slowed them down, and what would make their day easier. The answer was consistent: "We just want to stop chasing information."

That's it. They weren't asking for AI or some flashy dashboard. They wanted reliable, frictionless access to the documents and tools they used every day. That's what *value* meant to them.

So, we aligned our work accordingly.

This is where *Focus on Value* becomes a leadership habit, not just a principle. It means making value the litmus test for every project, every priority, every decision. Are we building what people need? Or just what's easiest to deploy? When you start any technology initiative in your organization, the first thing you should ask is, "How does this add value to the organization?"

We back that up with feedback. We requested regular surveys, focus groups, and post-project check-ins. Not to chase metrics, but to stay honest.

We used SLAs (Service Level Agreements) not as control tools, but as commitment tools. They helped us define what value *looked like* in specific, measurable ways. How fast are we responding? Are we solving the correct problems? Where do we need to adjust?

And we shared those results openly. Visibility builds trust.

Here's what I want you to take away:

You don't define value. Your users do.

Your job is to listen, align, and deliver.

That's how you build a reputation—not just as a tech leader, but as a *business* leader.

In our following letter, I'll show you why starting with what you already have might be the smartest move you can make.

Until then, stay curious, stay close to your people, and always lead with value.

With respect,

A Fellow Leader

Define What Matters

1. Where are you currently making assumptions about what your stakeholders value?

2. How do you define success, and does your team agree with that definition?

3. What is one way you can validate value before delivering?

Tools for Action:

1. Create a "value profile" template for each major stakeholder.
2. Set up a recurring 15-minute "alignment check-in" to refine success metrics.
3. Map each project initiative to a clear business impact statement.

Putting Focus on Value into Practice

Think about an IT service that your organization provides. How does this service contribute to the overall business objectives and goals? Identify how this service delivers value to your customers and stakeholders.

Letter 4: Start When You Are – And Win

Dear Fellow Leader,

Hopefully, now you are thinking more deeply about what it means to focus on value. That's not a slight shift—it's a sign that you're ready to lead more intentionally. And since you've gotten that far, I want to talk to you about something that's just as important: where to begin.

Not next quarter. Not after the next planning session. Not when everything lines up just right.

Right where you are.

There's this principle from ITIL that I keep coming back to, and I think it'll serve you well, too. It's called "***Start Where You Are.***" Now, I know—it sounds almost too simple. But in practice, it's one of the most profound and underused ideas in leadership and service management.

You'd be amazed how often leaders, especially the ambitious and well-intentioned ones, fall into the trap of assuming that change requires starting over. They see something broken—or just something suboptimal—and they immediately go on the hunt for a new tool, a better platform, a different vendor. They start bulldozing what's already in place, assuming that the answer must lie somewhere shiny and new.

I've watched this play out so many times. And believe me, I understand the impulse. New feels exciting. It looks like progress. It lets you pitch a vision that sounds bold and impressive. But here's the truth: new doesn't always mean better.

Sometimes, better means smarter. Smarter about what's already working. Smarter about what your people are already familiar with. Smarter about how to use what you have to solve the problem at hand without burning time, money, and trust.

Let me tell you a story from my own experience to show you what I mean.

At Aurora, we reached a point where people across the company were encountering the same issue: they couldn't find critical information when they needed it. Project updates, policies, and internal resources were all scattered. People were wasting time digging, asking, waiting. The frustration was real, and it was building.

Naturally, the first idea that surfaced was to create something new. A fresh intranet. Custom-built. Designed from the ground up. Something slick, modern, and tailored to our brand. It was tempting. Honestly, it felt like the kind of project you could put your name on.

But we paused. We took a step back. And instead of jumping straight into development, we asked a simple but powerful question: what do we already have?

Turns out, we had a lot.

We already had Microsoft 365 licenses across the organization. We had SharePoint deployed—even if it wasn't being used to its full potential. We had internal servers and communications channels. We had structure—we just hadn't optimized or unified it yet.

So, we started digging into whether we could use the tools we already had to meet the need, rather than building something entirely new. Could we design an intranet using SharePoint? Could we create something accessible, flexible, and reliable using the infrastructure already in place?

The answer was yes. After that realization, everything shifted.

We built the new intranet right inside SharePoint, using features that were already licensed, already deployed, and already integrated into people's daily work. We didn't need new vendors. We didn't need a massive deployment timeline. We didn't even need to schedule training sessions, most of our people were already using Microsoft tools every day.

What we did need was a clear structure, a thoughtful approach, and a commitment to solving the real problem. By starting where we were, we were able to deliver something faster, cheaper, and better aligned with our people's habits. More importantly, it worked.

That experience stuck with me. Not just because the project was successful, but because it reminded me how much we tend to overlook the resources already within reach. We often chase solutions out there when the starting point is right here. This principle—Start Where You Are—isn't about playing it safe. It's not about staying small. It's about being smart. Make decisions based on facts, not assumptions. And it's about recognizing that progress doesn't have to begin with a blank slate.

When you start where you are, you do a few things all at once. You save time. You stay within budget. You reduce resistance to change because your people don't have to learn something completely foreign. You build on familiarity, which accelerates adoption. This approach enables quicker delivery of value, as it reduces delays caused by lengthy implementation cycles or budget approvals.

But maybe even more importantly, this principle helps shape your mindset as a leader. It teaches you that you don't need everything to be perfect before you act. You don't need the best-case scenario. You need enough clarity to see what's in front of you, enough curiosity to ask what could be done with it, and enough courage to move forward without overcomplicating things.

I've seen leaders paralyzed by the idea that they need to get everything lined up just right before they can begin. They need to solve every edge case before they take the first step. But that's not how momentum works. Momentum builds when you make progress in real-world conditions, not theoretical ones.

So start by taking inventory. Look at your tools. Look at your systems. Look at your data. Look at your people. Ask yourself: What's already working? What's underused? What's being worked around? Where is there friction that could be removed—not by adding something new, but by using what's already there differently?

Suppose your HR team is still onboarding by sending email attachments. Before you go looking for an expensive new onboarding platform, ask: do you already have SharePoint? Microsoft Forms? Teams? Could you build an onboarding site with the tools you already own? Automate a few steps? Create a checklist? Embed content?

Or maybe your support team is drowning in scattered documentation. Before jumping to a third-party knowledge base, consider whether your existing tools—an internal wiki, shared drives, a tagging system—could be structured more effectively. Sometimes, it's not the tool that's broken. It's the way it's being used.

And I know you've probably been in situations where project management is a mess. Multiple teams are using different tools. Everyone is doing their own thing. It's tempting to buy a new system to unify it all. But again, what if the core needs could be met using Planner, To Do, and shared templates inside Teams? What if it's not about buying something new, but about setting consistent expectations and using the current tools better?

This approach doesn't mean you never invest in new solutions. Sometimes, reinvention is the right call. Sometimes, the thing you have is broken beyond repair. But here's the key: you only know that *after* you've assessed what you already have. You don't assume the answer lies outside your current ecosystem. You look inward first.

That kind of leadership—clear-eyed, grounded, resourceful—builds trust. It shows your team that you're not chasing hype. That you're thoughtful. That you're committed to solving problems, not just launching projects.

If you're unsure where to begin, just look around. Take stock. Ask questions. Talk to your people. Build small. Test fast. Use what you have. Deliver something that works now, not something that might work a year from now.

And then, once you've got that first win under your belt, you can iterate. You can refine. You can scale. But you'll be doing it from a place of clarity and momentum—not noise and guesswork.

In our next conversation, I want to talk to you about how to make this kind of progress stick. It's one thing to launch a change. It's something else to fully integrate it into your organization's core identity. That's where feedback comes in—and how you use it will determine whether your wins are short-lived or truly transformative.

But for now, sit with this idea. You don't need a massive overhaul to get started. You need a clear head, a curious eye, and the courage to trust that what you already have might be enough.

Start where you are.

Stay grounded,

A Fellow Leader

Start Where You Are

1. What underutilized tools or processes could you build on?

2. Where are you overcomplicating things in the name of "starting fresh"?

3. How can you pause and assess before your next project begins?

Tools for Action:

1. Audit your current stack—what's working, what's unused, what needs to evolve?
2. Run a "retrospective before the kickoff" to review learnings from your last significant effort.
3. Use what you have, refactor before you rebuild.

Putting Start Where You Are into Practice

How can your organization apply this principle in future IT projects? How can you ensure that your organization takes a realistic approach to change management and focuses on incremental improvements?

Letter 5: Progress That Sticks

Dear Fellow Leader,

Now that we've talked about starting where you are, let's talk about what happens next, how you keep moving forward without getting lost in the weeds.

The ITIL guiding principle **Progress Iteratively with Feedback** is your secret weapon here. It's about how you build momentum and ensure you're building the right thing.

Too many leaders set grand strategies in motion, then disappear until the finish line. Weeks or months later, they're handed a project that technically "meets the requirements," but somehow falls short of the mark.

That's what happens when you treat progress as a one-time leap instead of a series of smart, tested steps.

At Aurora, our intranet rollout exemplified this principle in action. We didn't build the whole thing and cross our fingers. We started small—with the framework, the home page, and one department's content. Then we showed it to the stakeholders. We listened. We tweaked. Then we moved on to the next piece.

It wasn't fast for the sake of speed. It was fast *because* we stayed close to the people who'd be using it.

Here's what progressing iteratively with feedback looks like in practice:

1. Break work into meaningful chunks. Think of your project as a series of small launches, rather than one giant release. Use an iterative method, such as Agile or Scrum. Each iteration should deliver something visible and valuable—something stakeholders can respond to.

2. Ask early, ask often. Feedback isn't a checkbox at the end. It's your steering wheel. Ask for it early—before you get too far down the road. Ask for it often, so you can keep adjusting.

3. Listen without ego. This one's hard. You might hear things you don't like. But that feedback is a gift. It's what turns "good enough" into "this is exactly what we needed."

4. Document what you hear—and act on it. Keep a running list of what stakeholders tell you. Track what you've implemented. Close the loop so people see that their voice matters.

The real magic lies in what happens when teams realize that their input shapes outcomes. They stop resisting change and start owning it.

Let me share a quick moment from Aurora.

One department head initially told us they didn't see the need for the intranet. "Email works fine," they said. But after seeing the prototype and realizing they wouldn't have to answer the same file request ten times a day, their tone shifted. They gave us feedback, saw it applied, and then became one of our biggest champions. That's progress, with buy-in.

When you progress this way, you:

- Avoid overbuilding or building incorrectly
- Save time by catching issues early
- Increase stakeholder trust and engagement
- Deliver value faster and with fewer surprises

It's also a massive morale booster for your team. They're not waiting six months for a big reveal. They're getting wins along the way—and staying connected to the mission.

One final note:

This principle isn't about going slow. It's about going smart. Iteration with feedback accelerates the right kind of progress, the kind that sticks, the kind that lasts.

As you lead your next initiative, remember you don't have to have all the answers upfront. You need a plan that leaves room for learning.

We'll dive into collaboration next. Because none of this happens in a vacuum, and no great IT leader builds alone.

Keep building with clarity,

A Fellow Leader

Progress Needs a Pulse

1. Where is your team flying blind on project status or outcomes?

2. What's one way you can share progress more transparently this week?

3. How often do you ask for feedback early, and use it?

Tools for Action:

1. Build a shared progress board (Kanban, dashboard, etc.) visible to all stakeholders.
2. Send a weekly "Progress Pulse" email with three bullets: what's done, what's next, what's stuck.
3. Add a 2-question feedback loop to sprint reviews or standups.

Putting Progress Iteratively with Feedback into Practice

Consider a scenario in which your organization is experiencing challenges with its current IT service management processes. Using the Progress Iteratively with Feedback guiding principle from ITIL, outline the steps you could take to improve these processes. Be sure to include specific feedback mechanisms that could be implemented to ensure continuous improvement.

Letter 6: No More Silos

Dear Fellow Leader,

You've probably already figured out that the success of any IT initiative isn't just about the code, the architecture, or the tools. It's about people. And more specifically, it's about how well those people work together—or don't.

In my experience, that's the line between success and failure. I've seen brilliant strategies stumble and stall—not because the technology was wrong, but because the teams weren't aligned, the communication wasn't clear, and the people who were supposed to benefit from the work never felt part of the process.

That's why one of my favorite principles in ITIL is this one: ***Collaborate and Promote Visibility***.

Now, I know. On the surface, that might sound like one of those friendly-sounding mantras everyone nods at in meetings but doesn't really practice. If you fail to adopt this principle, you'll face the consequences.

Collaboration isn't just about scheduling meetings or sending updates. It's about creating meaningful connections. It's about creating a space where people actively shape information, not just receive it. Where they don't just get tools handed to them—they feel ownership in the outcome. That shift—from passive recipients to active collaborators—is the difference between "meh" adoption and real, sustainable impact.

Let me give you a very real example. Back at Aurora, I saw both sides of this coin.

There was a time, early on, when we rolled out a system that had been developed almost entirely in isolation. The project team had good intentions. They were trying to move fast. They kept their heads down, focused on getting the work done. But they skipped something crucial: involving the people who would use the system.

When we finally launched, the confusion was immediate. Departments were caught off guard. Key use cases hadn't been addressed. Documentation was missing or unclear. Perhaps most notably, there was a pervasive sense of tension, as if the IT department had implemented changes without prior notification, requiring the entire organization to adapt quickly.

The result? Rework. Frustration. A hit to trust that took time to rebuild.

We learned from that.

So when it came time to roll out the intranet—a high-visibility initiative that touched every corner of the company—we decided to do it differently. We made collaboration central, not optional.

We started by inviting people in. Every department. Not just managers, but front-line staff. We held listening sessions. We asked open-ended questions: What's working? What's missing? If this platform could make your job easier, what would that look like?

And we didn't just write down the answers. We built them into the plan.

Throughout the project, we kept things transparent. We shared timelines, design drafts, and feature lists. We updated public channels. We ran Q&A sessions. We made it easy for people to see what was happening—and more importantly, to *influence* what was happening.

The feedback loop was constant. It was challenging, as people often held conflicting opinions and suggestions. But that was part of the process. It forced us to make thoughtful decisions, to prioritize with clarity, and to explain our reasoning when we couldn't do everything at once.

And then something amazing happened.

People stopped wondering what IT was up to. Because they already knew.

Stakeholders stopped feeling left out and started leaning in. We saw excitement. We saw teams sharing updates. We saw managers thanking us for including their voices.

Trust went up. Resistance went down.

That's the power of collaboration—not just in theory, but in practice. And visibility? That's what reinforces it. When people can *see* the work, they understand it. When they know it, they care about it. When they care about it, they contribute to it. It's a virtuous cycle.

Now, if you're wondering what this looks like day-to-day, let me walk you through a few habits that made a massive difference for us—and that you can start using too.

First, bring people in early. Don't wait until you've got a finished product to start asking for feedback. Engage stakeholders during planning to allow for flexible adjustments. It's when their input can shape the outcome, not just tweak it after the fact.

Second, use language that invites participation. Ditch the tech jargon. Speak in terms your audience understands—whether they're in finance, HR, or customer service. When people feel like they know what you're talking about, they're more likely to join the conversation and offer genuine insight.

Third, demonstrate your progress instead of just claiming it. We created a simple dashboard that tracked milestones, progress bars, key deliverables. It wasn't fancy, but it was consistent and easy to find. People could check in at any time and see how things were moving. That kind of visibility creates confidence.

Fourth, celebrate the small wins. If a department successfully adopts a new tool, highlight it. If feedback leads to a meaningful change in design, tell that story. When people see that their involvement leads to results, they're more likely to keep showing up.

Lastly, it is essential to create an environment where individuals feel comfortable expressing their views. Create a culture where honest feedback is welcome, even if it's critical. This isn't about pleasing everyone. It's about creating a shared space where dialogue leads to better outcomes.

At Aurora, we didn't just deliver an intranet. We built something deeper. We built a rhythm of engagement. We built a shared sense of momentum. We formed a trust that endured beyond the project.

You know what happened the next time we rolled out a tool? People didn't hesitate. They remembered how they were treated. They remembered that their voice mattered. And they leaned in not just out of compliance, but out of willingness.

This is the core of the principle. Not just getting better results today—but building the kind of culture where good results become the norm.

Because once collaboration becomes the habit—once visibility is expected, not exceptional—you're no longer pulling people along. They're walking with you. Sometimes even leading the way.

I want to leave you with one more thought. In leadership, it's tempting to think that our job is to lead from the front—to chart the path, make the decisions, and hope others follow. And yes, sometimes that's needed. But more often than not, especially in IT, your power doesn't come from being in front. It comes from being in the middle.

Being the connector. The amplifier. The one who holds space, facilitates dialogue, and makes sure everyone has what they need to succeed.

That's the kind of leadership that lasts. The kind that brings people together, not just to deliver a solution—but to *build it* with you.

As you continue, consider observing your surroundings and identifying opportunities to include additional perspectives. Where can I shine more light on the process? Where can I lead—not by taking up all the space—but by *creating space* for others to join?

What are considered the most effective IT solutions? They're not built *for* people. They're built *with* them.

In my next letter, we'll step back and look at the bigger picture—how holistic thinking shapes stronger solutions and sharper leadership. But for now, sit with this:

"Collaboration is your superpower."

Use it well.

Lead transparently,

A Fellow Leader

Collaborate Intentionally

1. Who is missing from your decision-making table right now?

2. What's one way you could bring more visibility to your cross-functional work?

3. How are you modeling collaboration as a leader?

Tools for Action:

1. Run a stakeholder mapping exercise: Who influences, who decides, who's impacted?
2. Schedule monthly "connection sessions" across teams just to align goals.
3. Make collaboration part of performance reviews, not just execution.

Putting Collaborate and Promote Visibility into Practice

Think about a recent IT project that you worked on. Were there any communication or collaboration issues between different departments or teams? If so, how did these issues impact the project's success? Using the ITIL Guiding Principle of Collaborate and Promote Visibility, describe at least two strategies you could have employed to improve team communication and collaboration. How might these strategies have improved the project's outcome?

Letter 7: See the Systems, Not Just the Part

Dear Fellow Leader,

Last time, we talked about looking around—about inviting others in, opening the process, and making work visible. That's how you build trust, drive adoption, and create meaningful collaboration.

But today, I want to take things further. If the last letter was about looking around, this one's about looking *across*—and *up*. Great IT leadership doesn't just connect people; it also connects systems, teams, timelines, outcomes, and long-term strategy. It thinks beyond the task at hand and starts asking how every action plays into the broader picture.

That's what the ITIL principle ***Think and Work Holistically*** is all about. It challenges us to stop treating IT like a menu of disconnected projects or a to-do list of upgrades. It pushes us to see IT for what it truly is: a living, breathing system.

One that operates across teams.

One that extends beyond rollouts.

One that matters to the business not just because it's functional—but because it's *fundamental*.

And here's the tricky part: when we forget that, things break.

Let me take you back to a phase at Aurora that brought this lesson home. In the early days, we followed the practices of many organizations. We moved fast. We focused on the immediate need. Departments approached us with requests, whether urgent or well-structured, and we responded promptly and efficiently. We'd work hard to solve that specific problem. And to be fair, we got a lot of wins that way.

But we also got blindsided more times than I'd like to admit.

We'd roll out a change that made life easier for one group, only to find it slowed down another. A new platform that worked beautifully in isolation created a ripple effect of confusion across integrated systems. We upgraded one tool, not realizing that three downstream teams depended on its original configuration. And because we weren't always asking the right questions, we'd end up in rework mode, trying to put out fires we unintentionally started.

We weren't careless. But we were zoomed in too close.

It wasn't until we *zoomed out*—stepped back—that those things started to change. Once we began seeing our work not as individual projects but as threads in a larger organizational fabric, our outcomes got better. Our systems have become more stable. And our people—both in IT and across the business—started working with greater alignment.

That's the shift holistic thinking creates.

You stop asking, "What needs to be done right here, right now?" and start asking, "How does this fit into the big picture?" You stop solving isolated problems and start building lasting, scalable, integrated solutions.

This isn't just a nice-to-have. It's essential. Because IT today isn't just a department that supports the business—it *is* the business. Every team touches technology. Every workflow depends on systems. Every outcome is shaped by how well you connect your architecture to your objectives.

So the question becomes: how do you *lead* with this mindset?

The first step, I've found, is connecting the dots. And I don't just mean mapping systems—though that's important. I mean helping your team understand how their work fits into the bigger picture. Not in vague, theoretical terms—but in specific, functional ways.

If someone is building an API, do they understand which departments rely on it—and how often? If someone is provisioning new cloud infrastructure, do they know what business functions that infrastructure is enabling? If someone's setting up a dashboard, do they know who will use the data—and for what decisions?

That kind of thinking doesn't just happen. Model it. Encourage it. Create space for it in your project planning, in your retrospectives, in your team meetings. Make it a habit to step back and ask, "What are we connected to?"

And once you start doing that internally, you also need to start doing it externally—across departments.

Because you can't think holistically without building cross-functional relationships.

Let me be clear: this isn't about collaboration in the abstract. It's about genuinely understanding what makes the rest of the business tick. It's about building genuine relationships with people outside your technical sphere—operations, finance, HR, sales, legal, you name it—people with their own goals, their pressures, their visions of what success looks like.

Get to know them. Not just when you need something. Not just when there's a project at stake, start showing up with curiosity. Ask what their most significant points are. What goals are they chasing this quarter? What changes are coming down the line?

The more you know what keeps them up at night, the better you can align your strategy—and the more they'll trust that IT isn't just reacting to problems but anticipating needs.

And this brings us to one of the most practical things you can do: plan *together*.

Integrated planning is one of the most overlooked tools in an IT leader's toolkit. Too often, we plan in our silos. IT builds a roadmap. Finance builds a budget. Operations create process improvements. And we only connect the dots after the plans are finalized.

But by then, it's too late to really sync up.

What happens when you bring everyone to the table earlier? Magic.

You get fewer surprises. Fewer competing priorities. More opportunities to share resources, align schedules, and pursue shared outcomes.

At Aurora, we started pulling more voices into our planning sessions—and I mean way beyond IT. When we were scoping a platform change, we had operations, customer service, legal, and HR at the table. Not as bystanders, but as active participants. And guess what? They brought perspectives we hadn't considered. They spotted risks before they became problems. They helped us design rollouts that worked in practice, not just theoretically.

That kind of planning leads to better systems—not just technically, but behaviorally. It leads to shared ownership. When people feel like they had a seat at the table from the beginning, they're much more likely to champion the change.

All these efforts—connecting dots, building relationships, and integrated planning—only count if you're measuring the right outcomes.

In IT, it's easy to define success as "the project shipped" or "the deployment is complete." But holistic thinking demands more. It asks you to track outcomes across the full lifecycle.

Did the system boost efficiency? Are people using it as intended? Has it reduced errors, improved reporting, accelerated onboarding? Those are the metrics that matter—not just whether the install went smoothly.

At Aurora, once we started measuring this way, we got a lot clearer on what success really looked like. We stopped patting ourselves on the back just because something was "done." We started looking at adoption rates.

Feedback loops. Long-term business impact. And when something missed the mark, we used that insight to improve—not to assign blame.

The results? Our intranet rollout evolved from being measured by uptime or migration to offering much more value. We integrated it into people's daily work. We made it easier to navigate across departments. We created tools that match how people search, share, and collaborate. It didn't just go live—it *landed.* And the organization felt the difference.

But maybe the biggest change we saw wasn't just in our systems—it was in our team.

When you lead with holistic thinking, people start to absorb it. They stop thinking only about their role. They start seeing how their work fits into a broader flow. They anticipate dependencies. They flag downstream risks. They ask, "Who else needs to know about this?" without being prompted.

That's not just good practice. That's culture.

It's what happens when systems thinking becomes embedded in how your team operates—not because it's in a policy manual, but because they've seen the value of thinking this way.

And let me say this too: thinking holistically doesn't mean you lose focus. You don't need to weigh every option before deciding. It means you lead with awareness. You plan with context. You act in alignment—not just to ship features, but to deliver meaningful, sustainable value.

Because in IT leadership, you're not just managing tools or timelines. You're managing tension.

Tension between now and next. Between stability and agility. Between what one team wants and what the entire organization needs. Between optimization and transformation.

And your job isn't to eliminate that tension—it's to navigate it. To manage it thoughtfully. To make trade-offs transparently. To keep your feet on the ground while still keeping your eyes on the horizon.

So zoom out. Look wider. Think broader. And ask better questions.

Ask: What am I not seeing? Who haven't I brought into the conversation? What happens not just when we launch this—but after six months, or twelve?

Because those are the questions that shape better systems—and better leaders.

And trust me: the more you lead this way, the more your team will follow suit. The more your peers will come to you—not just to fix things, but to *shape* them. The more your organization will see IT not as a cost center or a support function, but as a strategic partner.

That's where we're headed. And it starts with you.

Next time, I'll share something that might surprise you—one of the simplest, most powerful principles in the ITIL playbook. It's not flashy, but it might be the one that gives you the most leverage.

Until then, think big. Act in alignment. And remember—you're not just leading projects. You're leading systems.

Talk soon,

.

A Fellow Leader

Think Holistically

1. Where are your decisions creating friction downstream?

2. How can you break down silos in your organization?

3. What system-wide impact are you not accounting for yet?

Tools for Action:

1. Conduct a "systems friction mapping" session: who's blocked by whom?
2. Align cross-functional KPIs so teams win *together*, not in silos.
3. Invite someone outside your team to a planning session to observe and reflect.

Putting Think and Work Holistically into Practice

Your organization is currently experiencing a communication breakdown between different departments within the IT team, resulting in delays and errors in delivering IT services. Applying the ITIL Guiding Principle "Think and Work Holistically," develop a plan to address this problem and ensure that all departments work together to deliver IT services effectively.

Letter 8: The Power of Keeping it Simple and Practical

Dear Fellow Leader,

Let me start with something you probably already know deep down—but may need to hear out loud: if you've ever felt completely overwhelmed by the sheer complexity of IT systems, you're not alone.

Not even close.

I'd argue it's one of the most common and quietly corrosive experiences in tech leadership. We begin with structure and safeguards, but eventually things accumulate. Processes layered on top of processes. Dashboards feeding dashboards. Documentation for tools that were replaced three years ago. And suddenly, even the simplest decision—like updating a page or granting access—starts to feel like a minor expedition.

I've been there. I've watched smart, capable teams burn hours on things that should take minutes. They weren't disorganized; instead, the systems had become so bloated that the way forward was no longer clear.

That's why I want to talk to you about one of the most potent, underrated principles in the ITIL playbook: ***Keep It Simple and Practical***.

Now, don't confuse simple with shallow. That's a trap a lot of people fall into. Simplicity isn't about doing less for the sake of it. It's not about cutting corners or dumbing things down.

It's about getting to the *essence* of what matters.

It's about removing distractions so meaningful work can flow.

Let me tell you something that might surprise you. Some of the most impactful, celebrated wins I've seen at Aurora over the years didn't come from innovation in the traditional sense. They didn't come from rolling out new platforms or bleeding-edge tech. They came from simplification.

The magic didn't lie in some brilliant feature or shiny tool. It came from sitting down, asking the right questions, and clearing away the clutter until what was left felt obvious—inevitable, even.

Take the intranet project, for example. It could have been a monster. We had every opportunity to overengineer it. There were initial pitches for AI-powered knowledge graphs, dynamic content feeds, customizable themes, and deep integrations with every tool under the sun.

But we paused. We regrouped. And instead of designing something that *could* do everything, we asked one question: What do people need right now to do their jobs better?

That question became our north star. It guided all our decisions. From the structure to the interface to the rollout plan. Everything came back to that simple test: *Is this useful today? Is this helping people work smarter right now?*

That clarity changed everything.

We focused on clean, uncluttered design. Clear navigation. Fast access to essential content. And maybe most importantly, we simplified the rollout. One department at a time. One section at a time. We made room for feedback. We adjusted in real time. We didn't try to be perfect—we tried to be practical.

And that's where we saw the real payoff. Adoption was smoother. Support requests dropped. Teams began proudly sharing the platform. Not because it had a thousand features, but because it was intuitive. It made sense.

Now, I want to zoom out for a second and talk about why this principle isn't just good UX advice. It's a leadership strategy.

Because simplicity, when you lead with it, does something powerful. It builds momentum.

When you remove barriers—mental, procedural, technical—you create flow. You create clarity. And people start to *move*. Not because they've been told to. But because they can see the path, and it's obvious, and they want to walk it.

That's the kind of leadership people remember.

What does it mean to prioritize simplicity in practice?

First, you've got to *prioritize outcomes over process*. This sounds easy, but it's surprisingly hard in practice. We're all creatures of habit. We get attached to how we've always done things. There's comfort in routine, even when it's inefficient. Leaders must ask: *Does this step, report, or workflow add value?*

If not, why are we doing it?

Don't be afraid to cut things. Legacy steps that no longer serve a purpose. Meetings that produce more confusion than alignment. Documents no one reads. Challenge the idea that "comprehensive" equals effective. Sometimes the best thing you can do for your team is remove something that's slowing them down.

Second, *design for the user, not the system*. This one's personal for me. I've lost count of how many "efficient" systems I've seen that force users through four or five screens to get to a simple form. This approach does not reflect thoughtful design; instead, it demonstrates a narrow perspective.

Put yourself in the user's shoes. Follow the path they have to walk. If it's clunky, if it's confusing, if it feels like a maze—you've got a design problem. And it's your responsibility to fix it. Not by blaming the user, but by making the path more straightforward.

Third, and this is a big one: *make decision-making easier*.

We often talk about empowering teams, but we forget that empowerment requires clarity. If your team escalates every minor decision, they lack empowerment and act cautiously. And if every decision requires consensus from three other departments, you don't have a team—you have a traffic jam.

Simplify the decision framework. Give your team principles to guide them. Boundaries they can work with. Trust them with authority, and back them when they make calls. You'll be amazed how fast things start moving when people aren't constantly waiting for permission.

Fourth, *automate wisely.*

Automation is central in IT. But too often, we try to automate before we simplify. And all that does is embed inefficiency at scale.

Before you build that bot, or script that task, or integrate that system, stop and ask: *Is this process even worth keeping?* Strip it down. Cut what you don't need. Then—and only then—automate what's left.

In this manner, your automation becomes not only efficient but also highly effective.

Fifth, and often overlooked: *document with intention.*

Look, I'm not saying throw out your documentation. But I am saying this: 40-page SOPs that no one reads aren't helping anyone.

The best documentation is clear, concise, and easy to use in the moment. Consider utilizing checklists, playbooks, and short how-to guides with screenshots. Make the knowledge available when and where people need it—not buried in a folder they forget exists.

At Aurora, this approach didn't just help IT move faster. It changed how people saw us. When users experienced systems that worked *without friction*, they stopped seeing IT as a bottleneck. They started coming to us sooner. They asked for input earlier in the process. They brought us to the table because they wanted simplicity—and they associated us with delivering it.

In this way, simplicity leads to influence.

A moment that stood out to me? A senior leader pulled me aside after a rollout and said, "You know, I used to avoid reaching out to IT because I knew it would be complicated. I look forward to it now.

That wasn't about technical specs. That wasn't about shiny features. That was about *trust*.

And trust, as you know, is leadership currency. You earn it not just by being right, but by making the right things *easy*.

Now, let's not sugarcoat it. **Simplicity takes work.** Often more work than complexity. It's easy to keep adding layers. It's hard to strip them away. It's easy to build something comprehensive. It's much harder to make something that's obvious, elegant, and essential.

But that's why it matters so much.

Because when you commit to this principle—not as a one-off, but as a way of leading—everything starts to shift.

Meetings get tighter. Documentation gets clearer. Processes become leaner. Teams move faster. People stop surviving the system and start thriving within it.

And when your team sees you modeling this approach, they follow suit. They start asking better questions. They start cleaning up their work. They start designing with clarity in mind—the whole organization benefits.

If you or your team are experiencing challenges due to outdated or ineffective systems, consider this an authorization to seek improvement.

Cut the fluff.

Simplify.

Focus on what's truly essential.

You don't need to be flashy. You don't need to overdeliver. You just need to be *clear*.

Because clarity builds trust, and trust builds momentum. And momentum? That's what drives transformation—not technology, not tools, not complexity.

In our next conversation, I'd like to explore this idea further. We'll talk about what happens when you *scale* this kind of simplicity—through intelligent optimization, through intentional automation, and through processes that serve not just the system, but the people who power it.

Until then, keep focused. Keep it clean.

A Fellow Leader

Simplify to Scale

1. Where is complexity creating confusion for your team or users?

2. What process or tool could you eliminate, consolidate, or simplify?

3. How are you rewarding clarity instead of complication?

Tools for Action:

1. Run a "kill a process" challenge—what can you sunset or merge?
2. Replace legacy SOPs with one-page quick reference guides.
3. Recognize team members who simplify, not just ship.

Putting Keep It Simple and Practical into Practice

Think about a recent project that you were involved in that involved implementing an IT service. Reflect on the complexity of the solution that was proposed and implemented. Did the solution have any unnecessary complexity? Were there any aspects that could have been simplified to make the solution more practical?

Letter 9: Work Smarter – Why Optimize and Automate Matter

Dear Fellow Leader,

If you've been following along, then by now you've seen the real impact of simplicity. You've seen how simplifying systems and communication doesn't just make IT more efficient—it makes it more trusted. Simplicity drives clarity. Clarity builds trust. And trust makes everything move faster.

So, let's take that foundation and build on it.

Because the next step—the natural evolution of clarity and simplicity—is *optimization*, and once you optimize, the next step is *automation.*

Now, let me say this right up front: the ITIL principle *Optimize and Automate* doesn't mean we're trying to turn everything into a robot-powered factory. It doesn't mean removing people from the equation, far from it.

This principle is about **freeing people** and freeing your team from the repetitive, mind-numbing tasks that drain time and attention—allowing them to focus on tasks that need judgment, insight, creativity, and care.

Back at Aurora, this principle came into focus one afternoon when we sat down and looked at where our time was going. We had a gut feeling that we were wasting energy on the wrong things, but we didn't have data yet. So we asked the team to start tracking their recurring tasks—just for one week. No overthinking. Just jotting things down: ticket requests, password resets, file forwarding, form approvals, status updates, meeting prep.

What came back was eye-opening.

We realized that a surprising amount of time—hours, every day—was going toward work that could be described as "necessary, but not meaningful." It wasn't the kind of work anyone got excited about.

It didn't move the needle. But it had to get done. And because it had to get done, it was quietly eating away at the energy we needed for strategy, innovation, and problem-solving.

That was our turning point. We made a simple but powerful decision: *optimize first, automate second.*

That order mattered.

Because one of the biggest traps in automation is trying to automate a process that's already broken, taking this action does not address the underlying issue, which may lead to a quicker occurrence of failure. You take something that already causes friction and multiply its reach.

We reduced our speed. We resisted the urge to start scripting and integrating right away. And instead, we took a deep dive into understanding the work.

We mapped our most frequent workflows—not from a systems perspective, but from a human one. We asked:

- Where does this process slow down?
- How many hands does it pass through?
- Are there any unnecessary approvals?
- Do users understand the steps—or do they get confused halfway through?
- Are we duplicating work in different systems?

That's when we started to see the bloat.

One workflow—ticket triage for the helpdesk—had become an unspoken time sink. Tickets came in through email, through a portal, and even informally through Teams messages. Each one required a person to review, categorize, assign, and sometimes even rewrite it for clarity. That work alone could take 20 to 30 minutes per request, depending on how clear the original submission was.

So, we got to work. First, we standardized the intake. We created a structured form with fields for category, urgency, location, and department. We added simple guidance on how to fill it out. We tested with users and adjusted it based on their feedback. Then—and only then—did we bring in Power Automate to route tickets based on keywords and field selections.

The results?

The same triage process that used to take half an hour was now happening in **seconds**. More importantly, it was happening **accurately** and **consistently**. And our team was no longer spending hours each week on the manual labor of sorting and routing. They were solving real problems instead.

That's what happens when you optimize first.

Now, let's talk about how you can lead this way.

Here's how to make optimization and automation work **with** your team, not just on their behalf:

1. Don't automate chaos.

This is the golden rule. If a process is confusing, bloated, or poorly defined, automation will only magnify the mess. It does as instructed, only faster and on a larger scale. And that's not a win. That's a time bomb.

Before you automate anything, pause. Clean up the process. Ask whether every step is necessary. Eliminate ambiguity. Get alignment on what "done" looks like.

2. Look for friction, not just repetition.

Repetitive tasks are easy to spot. However, some of the most significant opportunities for optimization are often found in areas where individuals encounter challenges, such as delayed approvals, inconsistent handoffs, and ambiguous requirements.

Ask your team directly: *"What slows you down the most?"* The answers may surprise you. But they'll point you toward the friction points that are ready for attention.

3. Track your team's time and patterns.

You don't need a full-blown time-tracking app. Just ask everyone to log their recurring tasks for one week. Categorize them afterward. You'll start to see patterns. You'll begin to see duplications. You'll start to see what's ripe for streamlining.

This exercise alone can uncover dozens of hours' worth of hidden inefficiencies.

4. Choose tools that fit your environment.

It's easy to be drawn to new platforms, especially those offering automation. But most of the time, the best tool is the one you **already have**.

At Aurora, we used Power Automate—not because it's the flashiest tool on the market, but because it integrates with Microsoft 365, which we already used. That integration saved time and training. We weren't asking people to learn something new. We were helping them get more out of the tools they already trusted.

5. Keep humans in the loop—where it matters.

Automation should assist your team, not replace them.

Don't build systems that remove every touchpoint. Build systems that **handle the repetitive parts**, so your team can focus on the nuanced decisions, the customer experience, the creative thinking.

Automate reminders. Automate data transfers. But **leave space for human judgment** at the forks in the road. That's where people shine.

6. Review and refine regularly.

Just because something is automated doesn't mean it's finished.

Things change. Business needs shift. What was efficient six months ago might be cumbersome today. Make process reviews part of your culture. Revisit automations. Track their impact. Stay curious.

Optimization isn't a project. It's a habit.

Now, I want to talk about what all of this means for you—as a leader.

Because when you lead with optimization and automation, you're sending a powerful message. You're saying: *"I value your time."* You're saying: *"I want our systems to work for us, not the other way around."*

That kind of leadership builds credibility.

It also repositions IT in the eyes of your organization.

Too often, IT is seen as a cost center. A reactive unit. A team that fixes things when they break.

But when you optimize and automate well, people start to see you differently. They begin to understand that IT involves both stability and **scalability**. About building systems that grow with the business. About solving problems in a way that lasts.

At Aurora, something incredible started to happen once we got into this rhythm.

People began coming to us with ideas. Not requests—*ideas*.

They'd say, "Hey, could we automate this onboarding checklist?" or "Is there a way to speed up the reporting process for this workflow?" They started thinking in terms of improvement. Of iteration. Of systems that could serve them better.

That shift—from maintenance to momentum—was the biggest win of all.

Once your team and stakeholders see *what's possible*, they stop settling. They stop accepting friction as usual. They start asking, *"What else could we improve?"*

That's how you build a culture of innovation. Not through a single app or workflow. But through consistent, thoughtful, ongoing optimization.

Let me leave you with a challenge.

Pick one process this week. Just one. It could be something internal—approving time-off requests, managing a shared inbox, updating a status tracker. Or it could be something external—ticket intake, user onboarding, report generation.

Bring your team together. Ask, *"How could we make this smoother?"* Brainstorm together. Then take one step toward improvement.

Maybe it's simplifying the form. Perhaps it's removing redundant approval. Maybe it's drafting an automation flow. It doesn't need to be perfect. It just needs to move you forward.

Because small wins compound.

Minor improvements free up capacity.

Small changes create space for bigger ideas.

And that's what this principle is about.

Not speed for speed's sake. Not automation as a badge of innovation. But *stewardship*.

Stewardship of your team's time. Of your company's resources. Of your energy.

When you optimize and automate with care, you honor the people behind the process. You empower them to focus on the work that matters. And you become the kind of leader people want to follow—not because you're flashy, but because you help make the workflow.

But for now, take the next step.

Work smart. Stay human.

A Fellow Leader

Optimize, Then Automate

1. Where have you automated a broken process?

2. What recurring friction needs to be reviewed, not just automated?

3. Who needs to be part of the optimization conversation?

Tools for Action:

1. Map a process visually: what steps add value, what steps add waste?
2. Use automation only after a 2-step test: is it reliable and repeatable?
3. Create an "optimize first" rule: no automation without team agreement on current-state clarity.

Putting Optimize and Automate into Practice

Think about a specific IT process or task within your organization that can be optimized and automated. Identify the key pain points or inefficiencies associated with this process or task. Then, brainstorm potential automation solutions that could streamline and improve the efficiency of this process or task. Consider the tools, technologies, or platforms that could be leveraged for automation. Finally, create a plan outlining the steps required to implement the automation solution, including any necessary resources, timelines, and potential challenges. Present your plan to your team or colleagues, seeking their input and feedback on the proposed automation approach.

Letter 10: Why Purpose Changes Everything

Dear Fellow Leader,

This might be the most important letter I've written to you.

While frameworks can guide us and strategies can ground us, purpose is what makes it all matter.

This isn't a technique. It's not a methodology. It's a leadership lesson that has reshaped how I approach every decision, every project, and every relationship.

At Aurora, we spent years chasing the right systems, the best tools, the cleanest metrics. But no matter how well we executed, something always felt incomplete. Until one day, I asked the most straightforward question: *Why are we doing this?*

That question changed everything, not just for me, but for our team.

We weren't just solving tickets. We enabled progress and supported faculty, staff, and students. Empowering teams. And once we could see that clearly, our work took on a different kind of energy.

We were no longer managing IT. We were leading change.

Let me show you what it means to lead with purpose.

1. Purpose starts with vision

If you don't know where you're going, no roadmap will be of any help. Purpose gives your team a reason to care—and a reason to push through the hard days.

At Aurora, we embedded our purpose into every project brief: *"This exists to make information more accessible for students and staff."* That one line brought more alignment than any spec sheet.

2. Purpose strengthens culture

A strong culture isn't built by rules. It's built on shared belief.

When your team understands why the work matters, they show up differently. They speak up more. They take ownership. They support each other.

We stopped hearing, "That's not my job," and started hearing, "How can I help?"

3. Purpose keeps you on track

Without purpose, even great work can go sideways. You launch tools, ship updates, hit deadlines, and still feel off course.

Purpose is your anchor. It keeps your focus on outcomes, not just outputs.

When things get chaotic, it's what brings you back to center.

4. Purpose elevates every conversation

Purpose turns updates into stories. It shifts the conversation from "Here's what we did" to "Here's why it matters."

That resonates with stakeholders. With peers. With your own team.

It's the difference between being heard and being remembered.

5. Purpose scales leadership

When your team understands the mission, you don't have to micromanage. You can lead with trust.

A clear purpose creates clarity for everyone. It gives people the confidence to act independently, to make decisions that align with the bigger picture.

Here's what I know for sure:

When people believe in the work, they do it better. Faster. With more heart.

So, how do you bring purpose into your leadership?

- **Write down your "why."** Keep it simple. Share it often.
- **Connect every project to an impact.** Not just a task—an improvement.
- **Recognize meaningful progress.** Celebrate alignment, not just activity.
- **Tell richer stories.** Explain not just what happened, but who it helped.
- **Live it out.** Your behavior teaches more than your strategy.
- **Seek value.** Everything you do should lead to added value for the organization.

At Aurora, the shift occurred when we began discussing the people behind the systems. We stopped obsessing over features and started obsessing over outcomes.

That mindset turned IT from a service center into a strategic partner.

If there's one lesson I want you to take from this entire series, it's this:

Outstanding leadership isn't about having all the answers. It's about holding onto what matters.

Purpose doesn't make the work easier. It makes the work *matter.*

Lead with it. Speak from it. Let it guide your decisions and your voice.

Because at the end of the day, it's not the tools we build that define us.

It's the impact we create.

Keep leading with heart,

A Fellow Leader

Lead with Purpose

1. How do you communicate purpose in everyday decisions?

2. What story will your team tell about what you stood for?

Tools for Action:

1. Write a personal leadership mission—and share it with your team.
2. Start key meetings with a reminder of the shared purpose.
3. Align performance goals not just to output, but to mission impact.

Putting Purpose-Driven Leadership into Practice

Reflect on your personal and professional values and identify what truly motivates and inspires you as a leader. Consider the impact you want to make and the legacy you wish to leave behind. With these insights, articulate your personal leadership purpose statement—a concise and compelling expression of why you lead and the impact you strive to create.

Letter 11: The Leadership Flywheel

Dear Fellow Leader,

If you've been leading for any length of time, you've probably learned this truth the hard way: momentum is fragile. It doesn't show up overnight. It builds—or stalls—based on small, intentional steps. That's why I want to close with a tool that isn't just about action. It's about sustained impact.

The Leadership Flywheel isn't a checklist. It's a mindset loop. A system of thinking that keeps you moving with clarity and consistency. When you're stuck, it helps you get traction. When you're scaling, it keeps you grounded. It's not about managing the moment. It's about leading through it, over and over again.

The flywheel has five key parts. Each one fuels the next. Together, they create a rhythm you can return to anytime the work gets noisy, the vision gets foggy, or the momentum slows.

1. Define the Value

Before you act, clarify what matters. Not just what you think is essential, but what your team, stakeholders, and users need. This is where so many projects go off track. Value is assumed, not confirmed. We chase outputs instead of outcomes. We hit milestones that no one asked for.

Defining value means asking better questions: Who benefits from this? What changes when we succeed? How will we know it's working? When you clarify value, you give your team a shared north star. You shift from pushing tasks to pulling purpose. That alignment makes everything else easier.

2. Build with Visibility

People don't trust what they can't see. That's why visibility is your second flywheel turn. It's not just about posting updates or having a dashboard. It's about making the real work visible—the decisions, the tradeoffs, the progress, the blockers.

When you build with visibility, you create a culture of shared ownership. People feel informed. They see where they fit. They trust the process, even when it's messy. One of the simplest ways to earn credibility as a leader is to narrate the work out loud, in real time, and with transparency.

Visibility also protects momentum. It keeps teams from duplicating effort, guessing about priorities, or disengaging when things stall. When in doubt, show more, not less.

3. Simplify the Path

This is where authentic leadership shows up. Complexity creeps in fast, through process, language, structure, or even good intentions. And nothing drains a team faster than a tangled roadmap.

Simplifying doesn't mean dumbing down. It means cutting through the noise and focusing on the essentials, removing friction, and making decisions faster. The best leaders I've worked with aren't the ones who know the most; they're the ones who can make things make sense.

Ask yourself: What's in the way? Where are people confused? What can I eliminate without compromising quality? Simplifying is an act of generosity. It gives your team the gift of focus.

4. Adjust with Feedback

Progress isn't linear. It's a loop. And feedback is what keeps that loop alive.

Too often, teams wait until a launch or a crisis to gather input. But feedback isn't a post-mortem—it's a living part of the work. It keeps you honest. It tells you when to pivot. It invites your team to co-own the outcome.

Make feedback part of your rhythm. Ask early. Adjust often. Don't wait for perfection. Progress with purpose means making decisions based on reality, not assumptions.

One phrase that changed my leadership: "Here's what I'm seeing. What are you seeing?" That simple question invites dialogue. It turns hierarchy into partnership. And it keeps your flywheel spinning.

5. Model the Mindset

This is the multiplier. The part only you can own.

You can't delegate culture. You model it. You shape it by how you respond under pressure. By how you listen. By how you communicate when the stakes are high and the outcomes are uncertain.

If you want your team to define value, be the one who asks what matters most. If you want visibility, be the one who shares early and often. If you like simplicity, stop adding and start clarifying. If you want feedback, welcome it with humility. Your mindset sets the pace.

Leadership is caught more than it's taught. The behaviors you normalize become the culture you create.

Putting It to Work

You don't need to memorize the flywheel. You just need to move through it.

Use it to reset your next project kickoff. Or when you're onboarding a new team member. Or when your team is overwhelmed and unclear. Use it when things are broken. Or when they're growing faster than you can manage.

This flywheel turns faster the more you use it. The power is in the loop. Define. Make visible. Simplify. Adjust. Model. Then repeat.

You don't need intensity. You need consistency.

If leadership has felt heavy lately, I hope this gives you a way to lighten the load, not by doing less, but by focusing better.

The flywheel won't solve every problem. But it will help you stay in motion. With clarity. With purpose. With momentum, you can build on.

Keep it turning.

—A Fellow Leader

The Leadership Flywheel

1. What part of your flywheel feels strongest for you right now?

2. Where is momentum stalling—and why?

3. How will you mentor someone else using what you've learned?

Tools for Action:

1. Build your own "Leadership Flywheel"—sketch how each principle reinforces the next.
2. Schedule a quarterly "momentum review" to ask: what's working, what's next, what's stuck?
3. Write a letter of your own—to a peer, a mentee, or your future self.

The Final Letter: Leading Through Aurora – The Project That Sparked the Letters

Dear Fellow Leader,

Behind every principle in this book is a lived experience, and for me, that experience was the Aurora project. This letter brings everything I have written about the Aurora case in previous letters into a summarized, easy-to-digest letter

Aurora wasn't just a system overhaul. It was a full-scale digital transformation effort across a large, complex organization that had grown in silos. Like many IT projects, it began with good intentions: to modernize the infrastructure, streamline services, and better align IT with business outcomes. But like many IT projects, what we faced was far more than technology.

When I joined, the team was overloaded, stakeholders were frustrated, and momentum was low. People weren't aligned on what success looked like. Tools overlapped. Processes contradicted each other. And trust—both within the team and across departments—was in short supply.

We didn't start with a blueprint. We began with honest questions.

- What do our users need?
- Where are we overcomplicating the work?
- What would it look like if we simplified first, then scaled?

That's when the ITIL guiding principles began to shape our thinking, not as a rigid framework, but as a lens. We focused on value. We made progress visible. We worked iteratively and collaboratively. And we brought clarity to every conversation we could.

Each letter in this book originated from a real moment: a meeting that went awry, a decision that sparked momentum, or a conversation that fostered trust. We failed forward more than once. But through those failures, we built something lasting.

By the end of the Aurora journey, we had more than just new systems. We had:

- Clearer expectations between IT and business units
- A trust-based team culture that valued transparency
- Simpler processes that worked in real-world conditions
- Leaders who understood how to lead, not just manage

Aurora taught me that transformation isn't about replacing tools. It's about renewing trust. That's the heartbeat of every letter in this book.

If you're leading your own "Aurora"—or trying to steer your team through complexity—know this: you don't need a perfect plan. You need principles, people, and the courage to keep asking better questions.

That's where leadership starts.

—A Fellow Leader

Epilogue: You're Ready Now

Dear Fellow Leader,

You've made it to the final page, but you're just at the beginning.

These letters weren't just stories. They were invitations to think, to lead, to build differently.

You've seen how value starts with listening, how momentum is built one feedback loop at a time. How collaboration, simplicity, and clarity can transform even the most complex environments. You've seen how strategy becomes sharper when you think holistically, how trust grows when you lead with transparency, and how leadership scales when it's powered by purpose.

But here's what matters most:

You don't need a new title to lead. You don't need a bigger budget to create value. You need the courage to show up differently.

To listen more. To ask more thoughtful questions. To focus on what matters.

The world doesn't need more technologists. It needs more *translators*—people who can connect the dots between systems and people, between problems and solutions, between chaos and clarity.

That's you now.

Whatever challenge lies ahead, bring what you've learned here. Apply it with humility. Teach it with boldness. Share your story so others can lead a little braver, too.

Because that's what this is really about.

Not just building better systems. But building better leaders.

So go forward with empathy, with clarity, and with heart.

You’re more ready than you think.

With gratitude and belief in your journey,

A Fellow Leader

Appendix A: 30-Day Leadership Sprint — Put the Letters into Practice

This challenge is designed to help you activate what you've read, one day at a time. Each week builds on a different theme from the letters, giving you a focused way to apply the ideas in your context.

Week 1: Focus and Collaborate

- **Day 1:** Write down what value means to your key stakeholders.
- **Day 2:** Ask someone what "value" means to *them.* Compare.
- **Day 3:** Map out who your decisions affect—who's not in the room?
- **Day 4:** Identify one place where visibility is missing.
- **Day 5:** Share a progress update with someone outside your team.
- **Day 6:** Ask a teammate: "What's something I've overlooked?"
- **Day 7:** Reflect: What changed in how you collaborate?

Week 2: Build Momentum

- **Day 8:** Identify one place where your team is waiting too long for feedback.
- **Day 9:** Choose a tool you already have but underuse—how can you reapply it?
- **Day 10:** Cut one unnecessary step from a process you lead.
- **Day 11:** Try a "show-and-tell" in a meeting—what's working, visually.
- **Day 12:** Find one micro win you can celebrate today.
- **Day 13:** Share what you're learning with a peer.

- **Day 14:** Reflect: Where are you seeing more movement?

Week 3: Simplify and Optimize

- **Day 15:** Look at your team's tools. What's redundant or causing friction?
- **Day 16:** Pick one workflow to walk through—where does it stall?
- **Day 17:** Ask: "If we weren't doing it this way, how *would* we do it?"
- **Day 18:** Draft a checklist to replace a long SOP.
- **Day 19:** Cancel a standing meeting that's no longer adding value.
- **Day 20:** Identify one place you've automated too early.
- **Day 21:** Reflect: Where has less complexity created more progress?

Week 4: Lead with Purpose

- **Day 22:** Revisit your leadership "why." Write it down in one sentence.
- **Day 23:** Share that why with someone you lead.
- **Day 24:** Choose a decision you're making this week. How does it reflect your purpose?
- **Day 25:** Ask your team: "What do we *stand for* in how we work?"
- **Day 26:** Tell a story about a time your team lived your values.
- **Day 27:** Ask someone what they've learned from your leadership.
- **Day 28:** Reflect: How are you leading with more intention?

Final Stretch

- **Day 29:** Write a short letter to your future self about what kind of leader you want to become.
- **Day 30:** Share something from this journey with someone else, a teammate, a peer, or a mentor.

You don't need perfection to build momentum. You need 30 days of clarity and courage.

Appendix B: Your Leadership Credo — Define What You Stand For

As you close this book, you've reflected on stories, applied tools, and explored principles that can reshape how you lead. Now it's your turn to define what you believe.

This exercise invites you to craft your Leadership Credo—a personal manifesto to anchor how you think, decide, and lead.

Step 1: Reflect on Your Core Beliefs

- What do I believe about leadership?
- What do I value in how teams work?
- What role do I want to play in other people's growth?

Step 2: Describe How You Lead

- When I'm at my best, I...
- When pressure hits, I try to...
- I show integrity by...

Step 3: Capture It in One Paragraph. Use this space to write your Leadership Credo. Keep it honest. Make it yours.

My Leadership Credo:

____

____

____

Revisit it every few months. Use it to correct course when work gets messy.

This isn't just about what you believe. It's about how you lead from it, every day.

—A Fellow Leader

Appendix C: Team Workshop Guide — Bring the Letters to Life with Your Team

This guide is designed to help you turn the lessons from this book into meaningful team conversations. Whether you're running a formal leadership session or hosting an informal reflection with your team, these activities will help reinforce the core ideas of each letter.

Workshop Format Overview

Time Required: 60–90 minutes per session
Ideal Group Size: 4–12 participants
Materials: Whiteboard, sticky notes, markers, printouts of reflection questions or tools

---

Session Template

1. Opening Prompt (5–10 min)
Start with a question from the letter:

- "What does value mean in your role?"
- "Where are we showing progress clearly—and where aren't we?"

2. Letter Reading (10–15 min)
Please read the letter aloud or summarize its key themes.

3. Group Reflection (15–20 min)
Break into small groups and discuss selected reflection questions from the letter.

4. Tool for Action (15–20 min)
Apply one tool from the chapter to your current work. For example:

- Create a visibility board.
- Map stakeholders and identify gaps.
- Simplify a decision process.

5. Share Back & Commitment (10–15 min)
Each group shares one insight and one action they'll take.

6. Closing Thought (5 min)
Reinforce the purpose behind the work with a quote, question, or story.

Sample Workshop Schedule

Session 1: Define What Matters & Collaborate Intentionally
Session 2: Progress with Feedback & Show Progress
Session 3: Simplify, Optimize, Lead with Purpose
Session 4: Build Your Leadership Credo & Flywheel

These workshops aren't about perfection, they're about connection, reflection, and momentum.

Lead the conversation. Let the team own the insight.

Appendix D: Glossary — Language That Grounds Our Work

Agile – A methodology focused on iterative development, flexibility, and close collaboration.

Automation – The use of technology to perform tasks with minimal human intervention.

Collaboration – Working with others across functions or roles to achieve a shared goal.

Cross-functional – Involving members from different departments or expertise areas.

Feedback Loop – A process where outputs are fed back into the system for continuous improvement.

Governance – The framework of rules, practices, and processes used to direct and control an organization.

ITIL – A set of best practices for delivering IT services in alignment with business needs.

KPI (Key Performance Indicator) – A measurable value that demonstrates how effectively objectives are being achieved.

Legacy System – An outdated but still-in-use system that may be difficult to update or integrate.

Operational Efficiency – Achieving desired outcomes with minimal waste of time, effort, or resources.

Service Design – Designing IT services to meet the current and future needs of the business and its users.

Simplification – Reducing complexity to improve clarity and usability.

Sprint – A short, time-boxed period in which a specific set of work must be completed, commonly used in Agile.

Stakeholder – Any individual or group impacted by or with interest in a project or decision.

Strategic Thinking – The ability to plan for the long term and consider broader organizational goals.

Systems Thinking – Understanding how parts of a system interrelate and influence one another.

Technical Debt – The cost of choosing an easy solution now instead of a better approach that would take longer.

Value Stream – The full lifecycle of activities required to deliver a product or service.

Visibility – Making work, decisions, and progress easily seen and understood across the organization.

Use this glossary to stay grounded in the language that shapes your leadership. Clarity isn't just what you say. It's what people understand.

www.ingramcontent.com/pod-product-compliance
Lightning Source LLC
LaVergne TN
LVHW022013200926
848481LV00007B/2364
* 9 7 9 8 3 4 9 5 1 3 6 0 2 *